IF FOUND, PLEASE RETURN TO

NAME

CONTACT

THE 90 DAY SIDE HUSTLE STARTUP WORKBOOK & PLANNER

CONTENTS

ABOUT THE PLANNER...

Fear of failure is among the top reasons that people don't follow their heart and start the businesses they are passionate about. And with the failure rate so high for startups - somewhere between 50% and 80% by year 5, depending on which statistic you believe, it's easy to see why people are cautious. According to market research, there are 10 main reasons why startups fail, such as lack of focus, no market need, and this daily planner tackles every aspect head on.

Grounding your business idea in Ikigai - life's meaning - and combining it with the key principles of Lean Startup, this workbook and planner sets out the daily tasks to make sure you pick the right business, focus relentlessly on customers and test whether your idea will work, without spending much money.

By the end of the 90 days you will know whether your business idea will work and be ready to take the next steps to launch your product or service because you have proven that customers wand it and will buy it. This book gives you the steps, tools and motivation you need to start a business you're passionate about and turn it into a reality.

The front section contains the templates and tools you need to choose and develop your idea. Starting with Ikigai, you will make sure that your business idea is the right one for you and not just a money-making scheme that will leave you feeling unfulfilled. The market map, prioritisation matrix, business model and customer focus will make sure there is in fact a real need for your product. The resources at the back of the book include

- articles and videos for you to learn about Ikigai, Lean Startup and Minimum Viable Products (MVP)
- Ideas and prompts for emails and communication you need to have with your customer focus group
- Free apps you can use to get your idea off the ground without spending too much money

With a clear set of objectives and an organised, consistent approach you will soon have tested your business idea and be ready for lift off.

Let's do this!

13 weeks

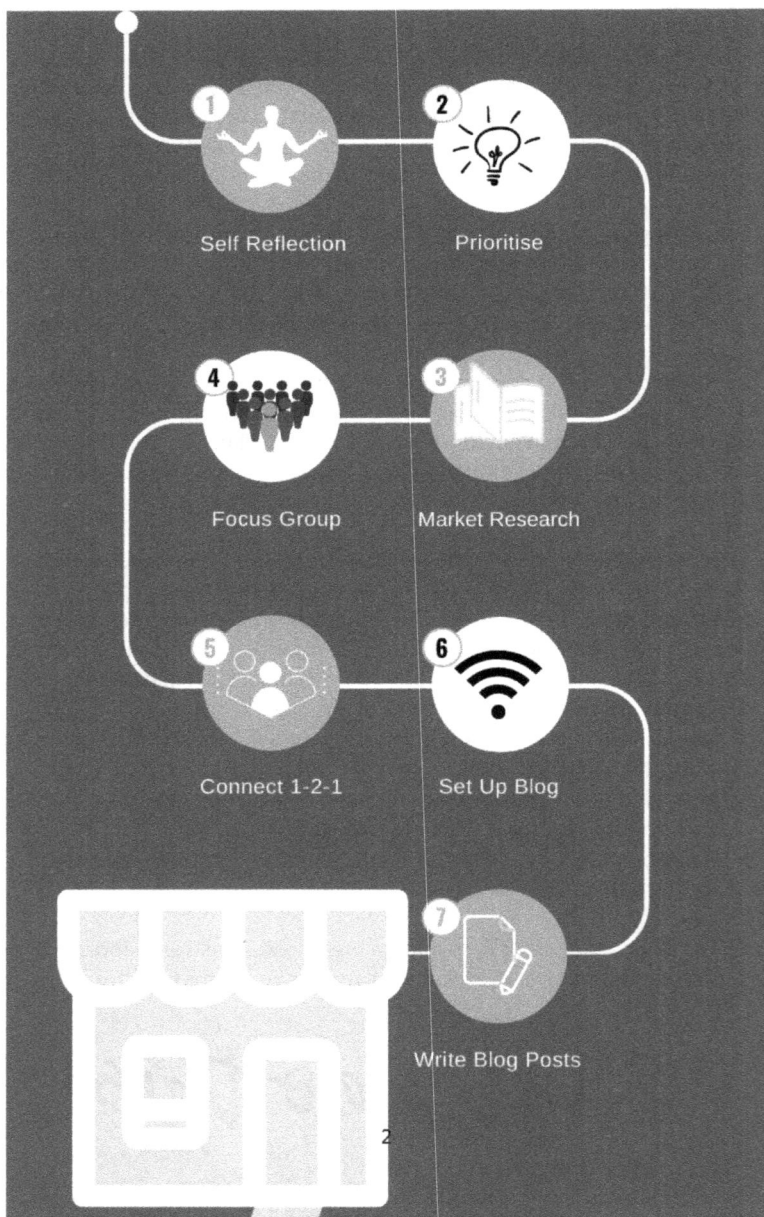

1. Self Reflection
2. Prioritise
3. Market Research
4. Focus Group
5. Connect 1-2-1
6. Set Up Blog
7. Write Blog Posts

to launch

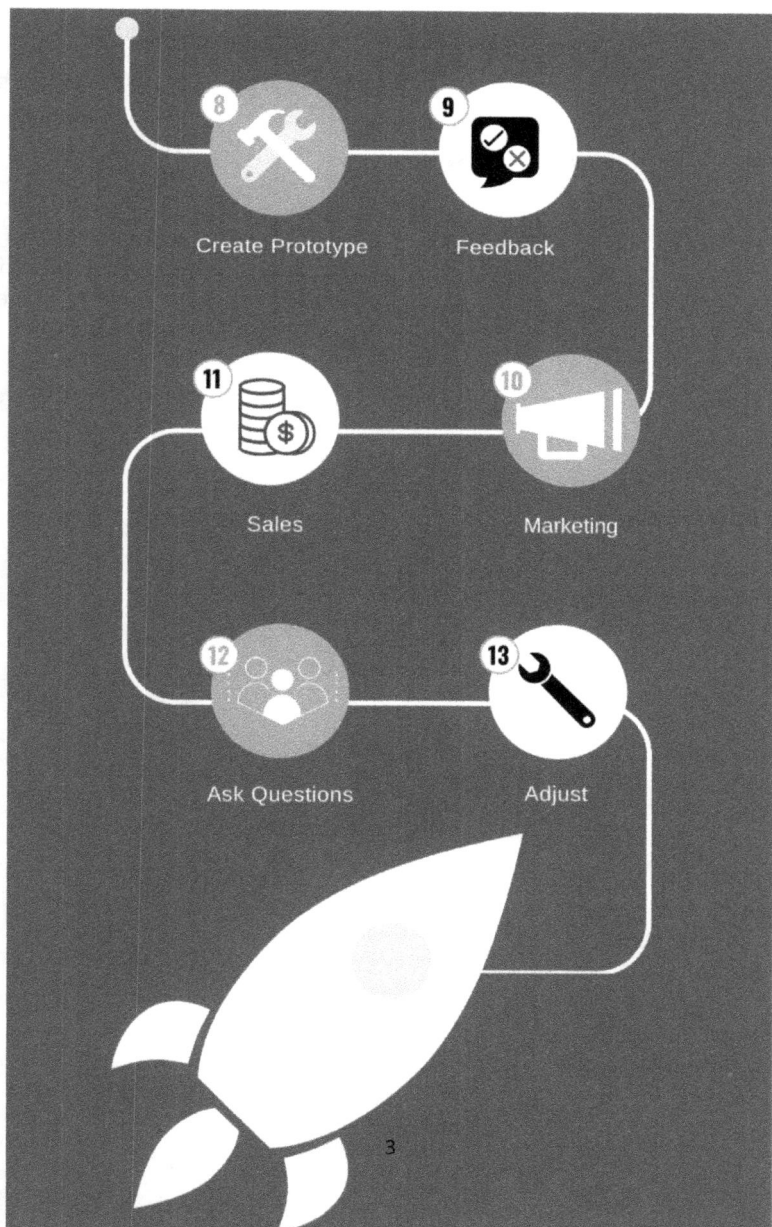

8 Create Prototype

9 Feedback

11 Sales

10 Marketing

12 Ask Questions

13 Adjust

3

FIND YOUR IKIG▲I

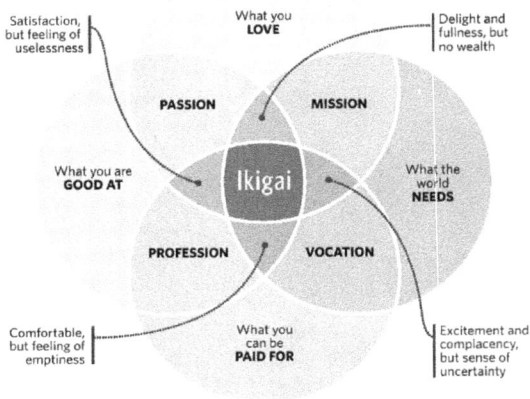

Satisfaction, but feeling of uselessness — What you LOVE — Delight and fullness, but no wealth
PASSION — MISSION
What you are GOOD AT — Ikigai — What the world NEEDS
PROFESSION — VOCATION
Comfortable, but feeling of emptiness — What you can be PAID FOR — Excitement and complacency, but sense of uncertainty

Ikigai is a Japanese concept meaning 'A Reason For Being'

It is a useful way to determine whether your business idea will bring you fulfilment.

What do you Love

Which activities did you enjoy doing as a child?

When you were a child, what did you want to be when you grew up?

What podcasts, magazines, and books do you read for pleasure?

Which topics do you tend to post about most on social media?

4

FIND YOUR IKIG▲I

What does the world need?

What personal challenges
have you faced in life?

If you had the power
what injustices
would you
eradicate?

What causes or
charities do you
(want to) support?

What are you good at?

What do people regularly
tell you you're good at?

Outside of work, what
are your hobbies and
interests?

What could you
spend all day doing
and not tire? What
energises you?

Ask your 3 closest friends
what you're good at?

WHAT'S YOUR BIG IDEA

Plot your top 5 shortlisted ideas into the prioritisation matrix

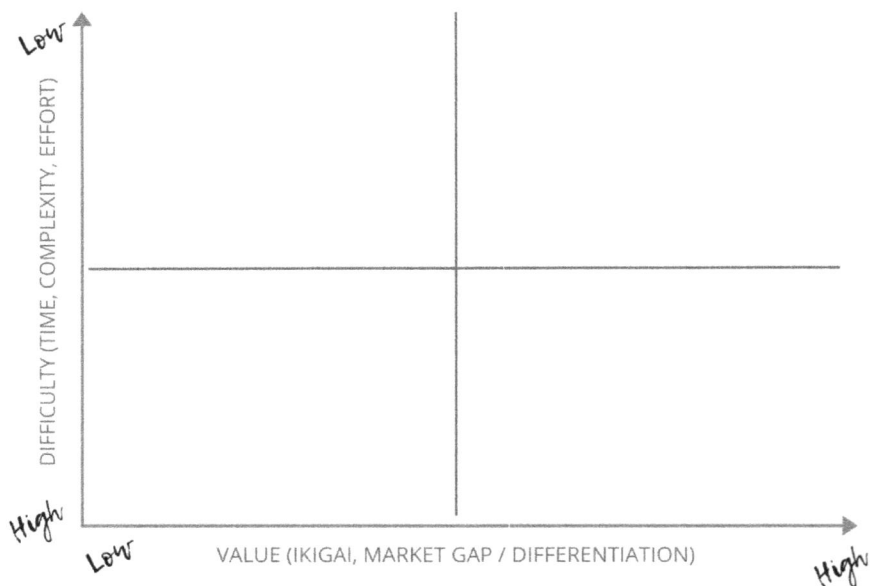

Low

DIFFICULTY (TIME, COMPLEXITY, EFFORT)

High

Low   VALUE (IKIGAI, MARKET GAP / DIFFERENTIATION)   High

Notes

MARKET MAP

Plot your competitor
products on price / quality

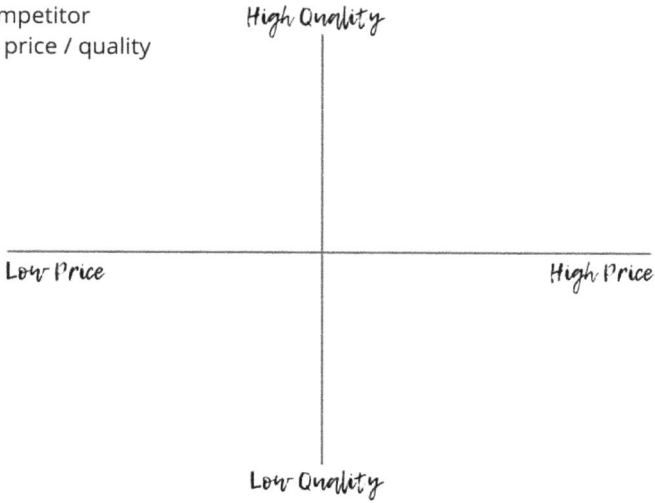

High Quality

Low Price

High Price

Low Quality

Plot your competitor products
on any other traits which are
important to customers

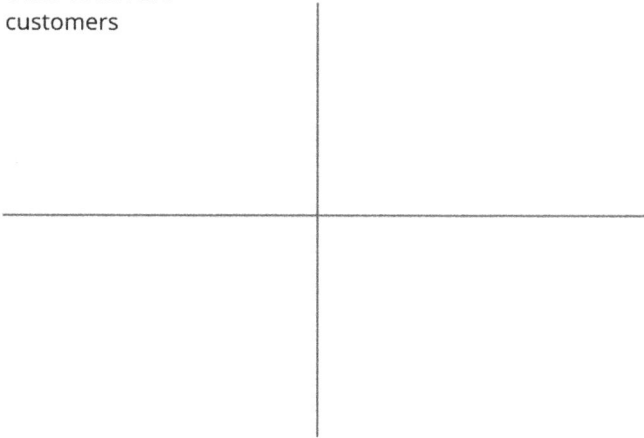

YOUR IDEAL CUSTOMER

Demographics: Age, Sex, Job etc...

Values: Beliefs, Politics, Goals

Shops: Where, what, how

Interests: Hobbies, Clubs

YOUR IDEAL CUSTOMER

Problem addressed by your product　　**How they benefit from your product**

Social Media preferences　　　　　　　**Info: Reads, Watches**

YOUR BUSINESS MODEL

What is your product / USP?

How will your product improve your customers' lives?

YOUR BUSINESS MODEL

How will you sell your product and for how much?

Describe the key resources, suppliers and partners you will need

NOTES

SELF REFLECTION

DATE:

To-Do List   **Key Meetings**

Review the 13-week plan pages 2-3

My motivation for today: An Inspirational Quotation...

NOTES

SELF REFLECTION

DATE:

To-Do List   **Key Meetings**

Read an article on Ikigai

My motivation for today: What's my WHY?

NOTES

SELF REFLECTION

DATE:

To-Do List   **Key Meetings**

Ikigai: What do you love page 5

My motivation for today: Which of my end-goals am I working on today?

NOTES

SELF REFLECTION

DATE:

To-Do List   **Key Meetings**

Ikigai: What the world needs page 5

My motivation for today: Who needs me on my A-Game?

NOTES

SELF REFLECTION

DATE:

To-Do List   **Key Meetings**

Ikigai: What you are good at page 5

My motivation for today: What results am I starting to see?

NOTES

SELF REFLECTION

DATE:

To-Do List   **Key Meetings**

Read an article on Ikigai

My motivation for today: What challenge did I overcome in the last week?

NOTES

SELF REFLECTION

DATE:

To-Do List   **Key Meetings**

Review your Ikigai circles pages 4-5

My motivation for today: How am I helping others this week?

NOTES

PRIORITISE

DATE:

To-Do List   **Key Meetings**

List your 10 best business ideas

My motivation for today: An Inspirational Quotation...

NOTES

PRIORITISE

DATE:

To-Do List   **Key Meetings**

Test your ideas against Ikigai

My motivation for today: What's my WHY?

NOTES

PRIORITISE

DATE:

To-Do List

Key Meetings

Assess 'doability' of each idea

My motivation for today: Which of my end-goals am I working on today?

NOTES

PRIORITISE

DATE:

To-Do List   **Key Meetings**

Shortlist your top 5 ideas

My motivation for today: Who needs me on my A-Game?

NOTES

PRIORITISE

DATE:

To-Do List   **Key Meetings**

Plot your ideas on page 6

My motivation for today: What results am I starting to see?

NOTES

PRIORITISE

DATE:

To-Do List   **Key Meetings**

Choose which idea to test

My motivation for today: What challenge did I overcome in the last week?

NOTES

PRIORITISE

DATE:

To-Do List

Key Meetings

Read an article on Ikigai

My motivation for today: How am I helping others this week?

NOTES

MARKET RESEARCH

DATE:

To-Do List   **Key Meetings**

Research your competitors

My motivation for today: An Inspirational Quotation...

NOTES

MARKET RESEARCH

DATE:

To-Do List   **Key Meetings**

Map your chosen market page 7

My motivation for today: What's my WHY?

NOTES

MARKET RESEARCH

DATE:

To-Do List   **Key Meetings**

Describe your ideal customer page8

My motivation for today: Which of my end-goals am I working on today?

NOTES

MARKET RESEARCH

DATE:

To-Do List   **Key Meetings**

Research your ideal customer

My motivation for today: Who needs me on my A-Game?

NOTES

MARKET RESEARCH

DATE:

To-Do List   **Key Meetings**

Finish ideal customer page 9

My motivation for today: What results am I starting to see?

NOTES

MARKET RESEARCH

DATE:

To-Do List   **Key Meetings**

Review your ideal customer

My motivation for today: What challenge did I overcome in the last week?

NOTES

MARKET RESEARCH

DATE:

To-Do List   **Key Meetings**

Read an article on Ikigai

My motivation for today: How am I helping others this week?

NOTES

FOCUS GROUP (50-100)

DATE:

To-Do List   **Key Meetings**

Join relevant facebook groups/forums

My motivation for today: An Inspirational Quotation...

NOTES

FOCUS GROUP (50-100)

DATE:

To-Do List

Key Meetings

Set up email capture spreadsheet

My motivation for today: What's my WHY?

NOTES

FOCUS GROUP (50-100)

DATE:

To-Do List   **Key Meetings**

*Ask people to join your focus
group via text*

My motivation for today: Which of my end-goals am I working on today?

NOTES

FOCUS GROUP (50-100)

DATE:

To-Do List

Key Meetings

Ask people to join your focus group (WhatsApp)

My motivation for today: Who needs me on my A-Game?

NOTES

FOCUS GROUP (50-100)

DATE:

To-Do List   **Key Meetings**

*Ask people to join your focus group
(email)*

My motivation for today: What results am I starting to see?

NOTES

FOCUS GROUP (50-100)

DATE:

To-Do List   **Key Meetings**

*Ask people to join your focus group
(social media)*

My motivation for today: What challenge did I overcome in the last week?

NOTES

FOCUS GROUP (50-100)

DATE:

To-Do List

Key Meetings

Read an article on Ikigai

My motivation for today: How am I helping others this week?

NOTES

CONNECT 1-2-1

DATE:

To-Do List   **Key Meetings**

Create a private facebook group

My motivation for today: An Inspirational Quotation...

NOTES

CONNECT 1-2-1

DATE:

To-Do List   **Key Meetings**

Invite focus group to join fb group

My motivation for today: What's my WHY?

NOTES

CONNECT 1-2-1

DATE:

To-Do List   **Key Meetings**

Call / message each person

My motivation for today: Which of my end-goals am I working on today?

NOTES

CONNECT 1-2-1

DATE:

To-Do List   **Key Meetings**

Call / message each person

My motivation for today: Who needs me on my A-Game?

NOTES

CONNECT 1-2-1

DATE:

To-Do List   **Key Meetings**

Call / message each person

My motivation for today: What results am I starting to see?

NOTES

CONNECT 1-2-1

DATE:

To-Do List   **Key Meetings**

Call / message each person

My motivation for today: What challenge did I overcome in the last week?

NOTES

CONNECT 1-2-1

DATE:

To-Do List   **Key Meetings**

Read an article on Ikigai

My motivation for today: How am I helping others this week?

NOTES

SET UP BLOG

DATE:

To-Do List   **Key Meetings**

Check out Blogger

My motivation for today: An Inspirational Quotation...

NOTES

SET UP BLOG

DATE:

To-Do List

Key Meetings

Check out Wordpress

My motivation for today: What's my bigger WHY?

NOTES

SET UP BLOG

DATE:

To-Do List   **Key Meetings**

Check out Squarespace

My motivation for today: Which of my end-goals am I working on today?

NOTES

SET UP BLOG

DATE:

To-Do List   **Key Meetings**

Choose a blogging platform

My motivation for today: Who needs me on my A-Game?

NOTES

SET UP BLOG

DATE:

To-Do List

Key Meetings

Set up blog

My motivation for today: What results am I starting to see?

NOTES

SET UP BLOG

DATE:

To-Do List   **Key Meetings**

Set up blog

My motivation for today: What challenge did I overcome in the last week?

NOTES

SET UP BLOG

DATE:

To-Do List   **Key Meetings**

Read an article on Lean Startup

My motivation for today: How am I helping others this week?

NOTES

WRITE BLOG POSTS

DATE:

To-Do List

Key Meetings

Create an 'About' post

My motivation for today: An Inspirational Quotation...

NOTES

WRITE BLOG POSTS

DATE:

To-Do List   **Key Meetings**

Create 2 posts about the problems
your product solves

My motivation for today: What's my WHY?

NOTES

WRITE BLOG POSTS

DATE:

To-Do List

Key Meetings

Create 2 posts about yout idea

My motivation for today: Which of my end-goals am I working on today?

NOTES

WRITE BLOG POSTS

DATE:

To-Do List

Key Meetings

Review and refine the blog

My motivation for today: Who needs me on my A-Game?

NOTES

WRITE BLOG POSTS

DATE:

To-Do List   **Key Meetings**

Share blog with focus group

My motivation for today: What results am I starting to see?

NOTES

WRITE BLOG POSTS

DATE:

To-Do List   **Key Meetings**

Request feedback from focus group

My motivation for today: What challenge did I overcome in the last week?

NOTES

WRITE BLOG POSTS

DATE:

To-Do List

Key Meetings

Read article on MVPs

My motivation for today: How am I helping others this week?

NOTES

CREATE PROTOTYPE

DATE:

To-Do List   **Key Meetings**

Review your business model p10-11

My motivation for today: An Inspirational Quotation...

NOTES

CREATE PROTOTYPE

DATE:

To-Do List   **Key Meetings**

Brainstorm MVPs for your product

My motivation for today: What's my WHY?

NOTES

CREATE PROTOTYPE

DATE:

To-Do List   **Key Meetings**

Read an article on MVPs

My motivation for today: Which of my end-goals am I working on today?

NOTES

CREATE PROTOTYPE

DATE:

To-Do List **Key Meetings**

Choose a low cost MVP to test

My motivation for today: Who needs me on my A-Game?

NOTES

CREATE PROTOTYPE

DATE:

To-Do List   **Key Meetings**

Design your MVP

My motivation for today: What results am I starting to see?

NOTES

CREATE PROTOTYPE

DATE:

To-Do List

Key Meetings

Decide pricing for your MVP

My motivation for today: What challenge did I overcome in the last week?

NOTES

CREATE PROTOTYPE

DATE:

To-Do List   **Key Meetings**

Read an article on MVPs

My motivation for today: How am I helping others this week?

NOTES

FEEDBACK

DATE:

To-Do List   **Key Meetings**

Create script for focus group calls

My motivation for today: An Inspirational Quotation...

NOTES

FEEDBACK

DATE:

To-Do List   **Key Meetings**

Call each person in focus group

My motivation for today: What's my WHY?

NOTES

FEEDBACK

DATE:

To-Do List   **Key Meetings**

Call each person in focus group

My motivation for today: Which of my end-goals am I working on today?

NOTES

FEEDBACK

DATE:

To-Do List   **Key Meetings**

Call each person in focus group

My motivation for today: Who needs me on my A-Game?

NOTES

FEEDBACK

DATE:

To-Do List

Key Meetings

Call each person in focus group

My motivation for today: What results am I starting to see?

NOTES

FEEDBACK

DATE:

To-Do List   **Key Meetings**

Refine your MVP and pricing

My motivation for today: What challenge did I overcome in the last week?

NOTES

FEEDBACK

DATE:

To-Do List   **Key Meetings**

Read an article on Ikigai

My motivation for today: How am I helping others this week?

NOTES

MARKETING

DATE:

To-Do List

Key Meetings

Create a zero-cost free giveaway

My motivation for today: An Inspirational Quotation...

NOTES

MARKETING

DATE:

To-Do List   **Key Meetings**

Create a zero-cost free giveaway

My motivation for today: What's my WHY?

NOTES

MARKETING

DATE:

To-Do List

Key Meetings

Send out free giveaway

My motivation for today: Which of my end-goals am I working on today?

NOTES

MARKETING

DATE:

To-Do List

Key Meetings

Write blog post about MVP

My motivation for today: Who needs me on my A-Game?

NOTES

MARKETING

DATE:

To-Do List

Key Meetings

Post details of the MVP in fb group

My motivation for today: What results am I starting to see?

NOTES

MARKETING

DATE:

To-Do List

Key Meetings

Email focus group to invite orders

My motivation for today: What challenge did I overcome in the last week?

NOTES

MARKETING

DATE:

To-Do List   **Key Meetings**

Read an article on Lean Startup

My motivation for today: How am I helping others this week?

NOTES

SALES

DATE:

To-Do List   **Key Meetings**

Take payments via paypal/stripe

My motivation for today: An Inspirational Quotation...

NOTES

SALES

DATE:

To-Do List   **Key Meetings**

Sales calls to focus group members

My motivation for today: What's my WHY?

NOTES

SALES

DATE:

To-Do List   **Key Meetings**

Sales calls to focus group members

My motivation for today: Which of my end-goals am I working on today?

NOTES

SALES

DATE:

To-Do List   **Key Meetings**

Sales calls to focus group members

My motivation for today: Who needs me on my A-Game?

NOTES

SALES

DATE:

To-Do List   **Key Meetings**

Sales calls to focus group members

My motivation for today: What results am I starting to see?

NOTES

SALES

DATE:

To-Do List

Key Meetings

Summarise common objections

My motivation for today: What challenge did I overcome in the last week?

NOTES

SALES

DATE:

To-Do List

Key Meetings

Read an article on Ikigai

My motivation for today: How am I helping others this week?

NOTES

ASK QUESTIONS

DATE:

To-Do List   **Key Meetings**

Email questions to focus group

My motivation for today: An Inspirational Quotation...

NOTES

ASK QUESTIONS

DATE:

To-Do List   **Key Meetings**

Use polls/posts on social media

My motivation for today: What's my WHY?

NOTES

ASK QUESTIONS

DATE:

To-Do List   **Key Meetings**

Answer focus group feedback

My motivation for today: Which of my end-goals am I working on today?

NOTES

ASK QUESTIONS

DATE:

To-Do List   **Key Meetings**

Email questions to focus group

My motivation for today: Who needs me on my A-Game?

NOTES

ASK QUESTIONS

DATE:

To-Do List   **Key Meetings**

Use polls/posts on social media

My motivation for today: What results am I starting to see?

NOTES

ASK QUESTIONS

DATE:

To-Do List   **Key Meetings**

Answer focus group feedback

My motivation for today: What challenge did I overcome in the last week?

NOTES

ASK QUESTIONS

DATE:

To-Do List   **Key Meetings**

Read an article on MVPs

My motivation for today: How am I helping others this week?

NOTES

ADJUST

DATE:

To-Do List   **Key Meetings**

Refine MVP and pricing

My motivation for today: An Inspirational Quotation...

NOTES

ADJUST

DATE:

To-Do List   **Key Meetings**

Create a zero-cost free giveaway

My motivation for today: What's my WHY?

NOTES

ADJUST

DATE:

To-Do List   **Key Meetings**

Create a zero-cost free giveaway

My motivation for today: Which of my end-goals am I working on today?

NOTES

ADJUST

DATE:

To-Do List   **Key Meetings**

Send out free giveaway

My motivation for today: Who needs me on my A-Game?

NOTES

ADJUST

DATE:

To-Do List   **Key Meetings**

Write blog post about MVP

My motivation for today: What results am I starting to see?

NOTES

ADJUST

DATE:

To-Do List   **Key Meetings**

Social Media update on MVP

My motivation for today: What challenge did I overcome in the last week?

NOTES

ADJUST

DATE:

To-Do List   **Key Meetings**

Read an article on Ikigai

My motivation for today: How am I helping others this week?

ARTICLES & VIDEOS

IKIGAI

Forbes
- Ikigai Is The Japanese Method Of Determining Whether Or Not Your Work Will Fulfill You, Mar 2019
- Discover Your Passion -- Or 'Ikigai' -- With 4 Simple Tips, Sept 2017
- How To Find Your Ikigai And Transform Your Outlook On Life And Business, Feb 2018

Business Insider
- The Japanese concept of Ikigai could be the secret to a long, meaningful life, Sep 2017

Entrepreneur
- The Meaning of Life for Entrepreneurs: Find What You Love, Then Share It, Jun 2019

Inc
- How the Japanese Word 'Ikigai' Can Help Your Business Be More Successful, Jan 2020

TED/TEDx talks
- How to Ikigai, Tim Tamashiro
- Don't wait, find your Ikigai, Gangadharan Menon
- Ikigai: The Secret to a Purposeful Life, Emily Bidle
- In the pursuit of IKIGAI, Marianna Pohgosyan

LEAN STARTUP AND MINIMUM VIABLE PRODUCTS

Forbes
- Think Like A Lean Startup, Even If You're Not A Startup, Jan 2020
- Entrepreneur 101: What To Know About MVPs, Jan 2020
- Want To Run A Lean Startup? Follow These 15 Money-Saving Tips, Oct 2018

Entrepreneur
- 4 Mistakes Entrepreneurs Make When Building an MVP, Jun 2019

Youtube Videos (titles)
- Validate your business idea: THE LEAN STARTUP by Eric Ries
- "The Lean Startup" by Eric Ries - BOOK SUMMARY

FOCUS GROUP COMMS

- Your focus group should be as close as possible to your target customer and be interested in your product area
- Wherever possible, make all communications as personal and relevant to the individual as possible, in your own friendly style/tone of voice.

Week 4 Focus Group Invite
- Hi [first name], I'm thinking of starting .... about....... and thought it might be your thing. Shall I keep you posted?

Week 5 Facebook Group Invite / 1-2-1 Calls
- Hi [first name], Thanks for getting involved! I've set up a Facebook group where I'll be sharing updates and asking for your help. I'd really love your feedback to make this as useful as possible. Please join in the fun?
- 1-2-1 calls are to say hi, pass on thanks for getting involved, and to speak to your focus group in more detail about the problem your product is trying to address

Week 7 Blog
- Hi [first name], I've set up a blog for the new [product/service] and would love to get your opinion. Please can you spare a few minutes to have a look?
- Hi [first name], Did you have a chance to have a look at the blog? Is there anything missing? Was anything unclear? I'd love to know what worked for you, but more importantly what I could improve on. Please be brutally honest :-)

Week 9 Prototype Feedback
- 1-2-1 calls are to say hi, continue to say thanks for getting involved, explain your prototype. Discuss whether they agree it meets the problem. Ask them what they would be prepared to pay.

Week 10 Marketing
- By now you should have a very good idea of what would be helpful for your focus group.
- Options: 'How To' PDFs, Cheat Sheets, videos; product reviews, industry reports, presentations, workshop, webinar, spreadsheet or progress tracker, plan / checklist
- Invite Orders: Hi [first name], Thank you so much for your help getting this far. I'm so excited to let you know that..... is now available. I'm taking orders via [paypal/stripe etc]... would you like to pre-order it today? I'd love for you to be in on this....

Week 11 Sales Calls
The purpose of the call is to say hi, thank them for their time and/or order, and find out why they did or did not buy.

Week 12 Questions
Based on feedback from the sales follow up calls, use emails and polls to clarify things about your product that might need to be changed

TECHNOLOGY & FREE APPS

Foundations
- Google Mail, Sheets, Docs, Slides (free, online applications)
- Canva (Graphic design app for regular people)
- Unsplash (Royalty free images e.g. for use online)

Week 4 Email Capture
- Use Google Sheets to set up a basic spreadsheet including name, email, phone number and any other relevant info

Week 4 Focus Group Invite
- Hi [first name], I'm thinking of starting .... about....... and thought it might be your thing. Shall I keep you posted?

Week 5 Facebook Group Invite
- Use facebook IF THIS IS WHERE YOUR CUSTOMERS ARE. Otherwise, consider other social media platforms, like Linkedin or Instagram

Week 6 - Set up blog
Your choice is down to personal preference. The leading platforms are as follows but there are pros and cons for each. The recommendation is to stick with a free blog site.
- Blogger (Blogspot) - free and owned by Google
- Wordpress - most popular blogging platform in the world; free site available and easy to convert into a full blown website
- Squarespace - not free but the easiest and best looking to use and convert into a full blown website

Week 11
Until your email subscriber list goes beyond 100, you should be able to manage payments and orders via Paypal.
Depending on your product/website you can investigate alternative payment options such as stripe.

www.ingramcontent.com/pod-product-compliance
Lightning Source LLC
Chambersburg PA
CBHW050532190326
41458CB00007B/1763